AF333558

**The
White
House**
by
Joel
Craig

for Daniel,

Grateful to share
the spirit, the
belief in the
potential of
poetry. Glad
to know you.

Kindly,

Acknowledgements: Thanks to the editors of these publications, where versions of some of these poems first appeared: *A Public Space, Boston Review, GutCult, Iowa Review, MAKE, FENCE, MoonLit, Rabbit Light Movies, Seven Corners, Spoon River Poetry Review, Van Gogh's Ear, The Zoland Annual, TYPO,* and *The City Visible.* ¶ Many thanks to Marvin Bell and the editors of Lost Horse Press, who published some of these poems in a short book, *Shine Tomorrow.* ¶ "Instructions for Building a Paper House," was created initially as text for a video collaboration with the artist Kirsten Leenars called *Instructions for Building "Paperhouse"*; special thanks to Kirsten. ¶ "Home With Light and Neutral Blossoms" was screen printed as a broadside by artist Jeff Evergreen for the Kalamazoo Book Arts Center series *Poets in Print*; special thanks to Jeff, Adam Clay and the KBAC. ¶ "Penguin" was printed as a mini-book storigami by Featherproof Books; special thanks to Zach Dodson. ¶ Vivid gratitude to Green Lantern Press and its wonderful, believing editors: Caroline Picard and Devin King. Thanks to everyone who conributed and gave invaluable support along the way, who are so many to name, but especially: Greg Purcell, John Beer, Michael Robins, Arda Collins, Chicu Reddy, Daniel Borzutzky, Adam Novy, Anthony Madrid, Ish Klein, Dan McCann, Nate Zoba, James Shea, Gabert Farrar, Peter Richards, Nick Twemlow, Andy Fitch, Chris Glomski, Ken Kordich, Ryan Kenealy, Marc Hellner, Lisa Janssen, Christopher Mattison, and Nick Demske. Chapeau to the *Danny's Reading Series.* A very special thank you to Kali Sullivan—hearts.

First printing 2012
Edition of 500
Special edition of 125 with screen print covers

Published by Green Lantern Press
1511 N Milwaukee Avenue, Second Floor, Chicago, IL 60622
www.press.thegreenlantern.org

Screen printed cover art, cover, and page design by Sonnenzimmer
Typeset in Alright Sans, Harriet
Typeface design by The Okay Type Foundry, Chicago, IL
Interior paper: Finch Natural
Printed by Book Mobile, Minneapolis, MN

For my family.

Tom Paine was sitting around trying to whip up a sequel to his last pamphlet, getting off the couch every so often just to pitch a fit, vacuum, maybe fix a can of soup. It had gotten to the point that Ruby Wednesday could barely look herself in the mirror, if she even had a mirror. No one was saying for sure. Then down at the Barnacle the neighbors suggested that Ruby might throw another one of her famous Tea Parties to cheer up the old man. "Right back at you," she murmured, but the invitations were already pretty much to hand.

By the time the President arrived, Tom couldn't count to ten unless a passing train roused him from his slumbers. Right at 1:20 the 12:20 cruised by. "I know you and you and you and maybe you," he roared, pointing out the judge and Greg and Ruby and Alex Chilton, "but who's this sickly stranger in the hat?" "That's not a hat, it's my natural hair," the President replied. "Oh, I get it, you come from out of the hazard zone," joked Tom, though even he didn't really understand what he was aiming at. In the next room, Keith Moon stared back at a plate of mashed potatoes.

The house was emptying out, most everybody on their way to a notorious dance hall. "You want to ask him something?" Ruby prodded the President, who was on the phone ordering a big brass band for the following afternoon. Tom meanwhile was indexing his vinyl. The President cleared his throat. "Let's stick to plain statements of fact," Tom said, grinning a little.

The President blushed; he knew when he was beat. He opened the closet door and out stepped the Vice-President. "So that's where you were hiding all along," marveled Ruby. "Sorry about it," the veep responded shyly, and then, accompanying herself on the zither, she spun a lengthy tale of woe. "I'm not a literary person," she began, and by the end of it no one needed convincing. Tom broke the frosty silence. "This was delivered for you," he told the veep, handing her a plain brown package.

"So you know about Joel Craig," the veep shot back. "I hear he's pretty tall." Just then the President snatched the package from her hands, ripped it open, and started thumbing through the volume within. "So what is this, some kind of poetry," he declared with a sneer. The light bulb blew out as if in spontaneous answer. "Mr. President, I reckon it's poetry, and a whole lot else besides, which is to say that this little book could transform your whole style of thinking, and not just your own but that of your fellow citizens, and I'm not saying."

Tom kept talking steadily in the warm dark, "poetry has some inexorable power, any more than when you're walking in an alleyway and hear behind the fence a party revving up that no one asked you to, except that when you turn the corner, it's your house that everybody's at, as the summer sun drops, and you want to know what separates that person on the other side of the fence, what made that moment part of you even in its distance, and anyway the facts are the facts: love and hate, war, political business. You think you know all about it, but it'll come back to you in a way you don't yet even know how to expect…"

Not that the President got small while Tom spieled forth, but when Ruby looked up, she could swear that she saw him tremble. Tom aimed for the rafters: "There's a spiral staircase in that book! There's sand and weddings! It's got subtle gradations of color in the pebbles! The food is really good: kale and tomato! There's the ineffable grace of seeming perishable! It's big enough to acknowledge possible let-downs! There's naked nightmares and beachfront riots! It's not afraid to explore the sexual! It seeks to describe! It seeks to describe! There's a goddamn WHALE FACILITY!" and finished up with some notes about process and "the arc of syntax, the arch of parataxis." He finished out of breath. "I've heard about enough. Get me out of this shitpile," snarled the Prez, now visibly shrinking. He leaned on the veep as they tottered out, her returning the book, "I think we'll wait for the remix."

Ruby looked straight at where her reflection would be if the lights were on and she had a mirror. She felt glad for no exact reason. Somewhere close Tom Paine laughed a dark dry laugh: "I guess they'll have to figure out for themselves—it might all still be called Chicago, California, the White House, the United States. But from here on out, it'll be the Joel Craig remix."

CONTENTS

> **"**What's obvious to me isn't always
> obvious to other people.**"**
>
> **— MIKE WATT**

> **"**The past is the one thing we are not prisoners of. We
> can do with the past exactly what we wish. What we
> can't do is to change its consequences.**"**
>
> **— JOHN BERGER**

pause

SCHEMA

He was born as his name implies
as though distortion weren't enough
in itself to frighten good, innocent people.
Even little children utter bold words,
but that's not the half.
There remains an apology that is due.
How necessary it is we keep secrets.
And what is to be done
to prevent something awful from happening —
or perhaps we just get used to it.
If momentum can do so much,
just imagine what it will do for us.

CALIFORNIA POEM

What is needed is a recognizable molecule that carries the unstable
                              promise to the brain. A good-humored Buddha
                              area of the self.

I've tried and tried but it keeps slipping away. We stopped
                              at a spot overlooking the bay
                              at the same time both observing and performing.

After the patrolman followed us we joked about dodging a bullet,
                              the first stirrings of pleasant feelings evident
                              without introspective urges.

Afterward, sleeping was tricky but it worked out okay.
                              I said thank you but I have to go
                              on with the rest of my life.

It's simple, I think. I open my mouth to say just that, but everyone
                              says something along these lines,
                              seeing places and things with their eyes closed.

A clear vision of big cities as actors in their own right.
                              When I close my eyes the first stirrings of
                              pleasant feelings become evident.

I rise and lead the way through the kitchen and dining room
                              and down the hallway to the bedroom,
                              feeling solidly connected to the physical world.

A good-humored Buddha area of the self. I spend the night
                              on a pad in their bedroom, for once
                              tired despite the music, the air clean and cool.

The piano plays on, undeterred, and in my place on the floor
                              I imagine my preferred self-image
                              awakening to clinical sunshine.

It's yet another distraction. How fast do you hold to yourself,
                    saying tiresome truths over and over again
                    to the tired people who rush into your life.

Have you ever been to Death Valley? I've wanted to see it for years
                    but haven't yet had the chance.
                    There are personalities you never forget.

We packed the car with sandwiches and the makings of a good salad.
                    The idea appealed to everyone.
                    For the first time I missed the road.

At the entrance, a small sign nailed to a telephone pole announced
                    FRESH OYSTERS FOR SALE, as if I'd built
                    an imaginary destination in my mind.

What will operate against a swift frame is a certain coolness in the work.
                    When we walked into the living room
                    my chest tightened, though I knew what to expect.

So far it wasn't at all like my fantasy. The kitchen was comfortably large,
                    with a linoleum floor so old its original pattern
                    was lost in a general brown-ness.

He led me down the hall and out the back door. We walked along
                    a narrow dirt path, past clumps of early narcissus,
                    under buckeye and pine trees.

One scene in particular stays with me. The hero has wandered
                    into a valley where he sees, all around him,
                    plants thrusting up by the tens of thousands.

For most of my life, whenever I was being introduced to a roomful
                    of people I didn't know, the tiny muscles on either side
                    of my mouth would go into twitching spasms

if I tried to maintain a smile. Noise erupted around the table.
Names of people and places I didn't recognize
were flying everywhere. Outside was the green world.

CHAIRS MISSING

History isn't clear. In other words
if the child is taught with love and respect
by wise teachers, the portals of heaven
open. You can fly up
over the top of the volcano like a bird
and look down on it. Beautiful
eyes that really see you.

The wonder of the world is ever present.
Tell me when you get there.

— in memory of Terry Ray Craig, 1959 – 2008

STREET DAD

Let me try to lay out what I think I understand
                      about my life. I took a sip
                      of wine and plunged.

The new plague has worked so quickly we've returned
                      nearly to equilibrium.

What's behind me has been built out of nothing
                      into a whole row of apartments
                      full of exotic people.

You can presume relative safety. I'm a quiet person.
                      I don't make a lot of noise
                      in public.

The most I can ever do is establish what appears to be
                      a relatively safe level
                      for myself, for my own body and mind.

A flash of amusement, realizing the invitation
                      to pounce could be taken
                      more than one way.

I have two cats who live outside, hunting gophers and mice.
                      There's a bit more to climb
                      until we level out.

She was thin, shy and tended to be exacting and impatient,
                      but I was a good, caring father.

He had the heart and clearness of mind
                      to be a therapist. We could afford
                      little in the way of school.

Emptying his pockets we came across a policy
                         for trying out new groups of people. A safe level
                         for particular bodies, nervous systems
                         and private individuals with questions.

They may be a bit uncomfortable about what
                         they think I'm doing
                         but they've no reason to stop me.

I used to have a dog called Bruno
                         but when he died I didn't
                         have the heart to replace him.

I learned what it was to be really poor, what it does
                         to the human spirit.

Fundamental things still apply —
                         a greenness that makes Ireland
                         look gray encircling a perfect crescent bay.

A place in which only self-deluded, naïve people hope
                         for things to get better. Las Vegas
                         and the end of Western history.

Above all is the ghost of sunk capital. Terrible assets
                         that won't be born. Telling a cop
                         to fuck off.

It's a strange feeling to look up the hill, across the grass, and see
                         those buildings staring down
                         where there used to be nothing but sky and trees.

She never really said anything I could count on, and I didn't want to
                         waste any more time or energy
                         than I had to on people who play games.

So to you, yes. Yes for telling the truth. To your intuitive fingers
                              and all the rest of you, what are you
                              trying to say?

She'll be coming to be with me for a while. I'm meeting her plane
                              tomorrow morning.

She's wonderfully gentle. Down the stairs into the living room, the fire
                              is still throwing off occasional sparks.

Lit fingertips move thoughtfully
                              up over the top of my shoulder
                              and pause behind my ear.

Do cities decay differently in the New World?
                              There's a faint touch of tease here — biological
                              warfare sort of stuff. Recreation crisis.

Keep silent in deference to the possibly
                              imminent end of the human race.
                              Seem comfortably at ease with private images.

Of course there are different ways to terrorize
                              from the sky.

If he's the kind that gets easily irritated,
                              I'll likely find out now.

Evolution rapidly manufactures new species or subspecies
                              out of their domesticates.

I didn't know I was suffering from an illness
                              known as depression. For the first time
                              in my life, I thought I was seeing the world.

I sat for a moment, staring at my knees as I tried
                    to put broad, wide images
                    into small, tidy words.

SO FAR SO NORTH

He doesn't know they are great but he intends
                    to give them a chance to be great.

Don't understand him precipitously. It is absurd
                    to describe the necessities of our educations.

Electricity flows to involve us in the depth in certain things.

One yearns to see a picture do its work.

Had I arrived two days earlier, from his description
                    it would have qualified as human experience.

From the point of view of accomplishment
                    and with a sigh of relief in a sea of gloom,
                    the voice this year is distinctly louder. The patient too
                    is doing well, much of her time on an ever more
                    worldly circuit.

The summer a host of us motored up for another look,
                    I like that, she said to the first one,
                    and that I like.

With circulation of image comes the shock of the assembled moment.

Rather than listen to her I'm making my way and cannot explain
                    any other way. I have this to say
                    but I don't quite dare.

STARS AS EYES

He is alive but something in his interior has been damaged. It seems
                                obvious now as we rub our eyes —
                                very often the truth of the new succeeds
                                in destroying the discoverer physically.

I could go to her house but I'm afraid of what I might find. I sidestep
                                the explanatory conversation, just a plain
                                Saturday night. Presenting a succession of facts
                                she is surprised by her inability to explain
                                why she must go. Both inward and outward
                                consciousness leaks like a house.

We are also great believers in hazard zoning. Only after
                                the celebrations of homecoming are over
                                can the real story of our lives begin.

My sister wanted me to meet her in Austin but flights to L.A.
                                were much cheaper. After the hearing
                                we went back to the hotel for lunch.

Experience must be related, retained and repeated passing directly
                                from one individual to another, and another
                                as playback takes shape on the horizon.

The air was warm. There were large yellow lilies spotted with brown,
                                and tiny scarlet blossoms on a black vine that wound
                                through and around a fence climbing the bank behind us.

In a seamless continuity of surveillance over daily routine, I hope
                                you'll be able to sit it out and forgive
                                whatever I said that might have hurt you.

Adjusting our point of view we are also great believers. Difficult talks
                    with friends about what is happening
                    to friendship. One has occasionally to hand out
                    bitter pills.

Speaking, however, from a distance that is steadily expanding,
                    a certain sadness inevitably creeps back in.
                    I haven't been with her for a while. There seemed
                    no way out of it, so I told her.

I sent you, some time ago, a letter which was very hard to write. Around us,
                    in what looked like the light of early morning,
                    was an abundance of flowers and leaves.

The picture that I love best, the one that moves me most,
                    shows the head of a big, dark green dragon. Its mouth
                    is open — and curled up on the big, red tongue
                    is a tiny baby, sound asleep.

The perfect part of work is technical.
Cataclysm charges the atmosphere.
It always does. The world
with recurring aspirations for wilderness
shakes down the housetops.
Here in the vision
it is a nice, sunny afternoon.
Because he could see himself getting raked
on every side, it is difficult
to imagine how people for years to come
will care for such refinement,
desiring everything.

SIGNS OF GOOD HUMOR

The little room
is always a little
dirty. The frozen north
we take to be a plain
statement of fact. Pre-
formulated as the backdrop,
good humor erupts
puzzling over
the question as to
why in the house
of dread, cleverness
and strangeness
are acknowledged
with gratitude —
a brilliant light as from
a calcium in a theater
beats upon the far
corner of the domicile.
The sense of space
and loneliness upon
the sea is all I get.
From an upper
window a woman,
instead of focusing,
bends, her tumbling
hair only sufficient —
only sufficient touches
the troubles of a man
and woman and the calcium
light upon the house
scarcely awakens
my interest.

I was handed a rose and asked if I could hurt it. In 1980,
                           here I am with the experience
                           dramatically fresh in my mind,
                           a burning desire to explain myself.
                           So this is where I started.

I had two babysitters.

I was handed a rose and asked if I could hurt it. I was handed a rose
                           and asked if I could hurt it.

Here I will describe briefly something called the alert.
                           Knowing that it's up to me to break the silence
                           I have started to do whatever it takes
                           to become expert. In the meantime
                           there is no completely safe procedure
                           if you intend them to continue
                           being alive.

Some small sign serving to remind me
                           this is a separate and very special category,
                           a mystical or even religious experience
                           which will never be forgotten, bringing about
                           a deep change of perspective or life direction
                           in the person who is graced with it. Answering
                           the phone is out of the question.

"Recalibration is a process that I do periodically.
                           My earlier experiments had been full of beauty
                           and light, and I rejoiced at what my soul contained,
                           aware of the considerable body, strongly colored
                           by attitudes and interpretations." He went on to convey
                           the magnificence of the theater, the deep blue
                           of the velvet curtains, the superb stage lighting and scenery.

I paid attention and chose my words carefully, no
                    mystifications, no confusion to the eye, no
                    gadgetry clutter.

He knows how to do what he sets out to do
                with perfectly obvious procedure. The sea
                is dark and forbidding. The horizon
                is dark and forbidding.

Even from a distance, the less said the better. The colors in some of these landscapes
                are perfectly desperate.

In a portrait there is never anything wrong
                with the mouth. There is never anything wrong
                with anything. Machines are not choosers.
                The next best things are certain. Heaven
                knowing the next best things. The young
                can explain it, but who would they explain
                it to? More promise than performance
                as all sorts of things begin to interfere.

An energetic hostess seated me at the counter
                next to a beautiful woman. It is possible
                the timid portion of the population
                unless held firmly in check will imitate
                the silliness of timid people of years ago.

Supplication is valued. As soon as I learned the facts I gave up
                on the exchange. She wanted something
                mysterious, as if everything were the same.

Life changes and so-called truth changes with it. The businesslike
                haste of the surgeon as he scolds the public.
                To look at him and the thing he can never look at
                shudderingly as the blood is drawn
                is the duty of every patriot.

In a constructive age such as this I should have neglected everything
                    for the supreme duty of aiding
                    in the reconstruction.

I took my courage, which starts everywhere and goes
                    nowhere, and spoke to her. Here
                    one can unquestionably infer the inside
                    from the outside.

The leaders of the free world, assembled as if by magic,
                    seem to have the enemy at their mercy.
                    It can be argued that Christ himself spoke
                    to the mob. The crowd will stop
                    to see almost anything. The crowd will stop
                    to see something about almost everything.

YANKEE CAN-DO

A body sure does get around.
Just one month ago I was riding Labrador

retrievers out the kitchen door of my hostess's
bungalow, taking blame for chewed sandals, and now here it is
lovely antiguaguat, what with 500-year-old church ruins and fettuccine

with truffle sauce and a post-

prandial snifter of grappa.
Needless to say, the philosophy is of death. Technology

ripening in the forest
undoes God's mysteries. How even the lemons
appear anguished; needless to say, no longer

need we unbury the pre-Cambrian evidence. One can learn

to be satisfied with an empty breath, the blue familiarity of sleep.
Another drink to again enact the mouth of October, the universe

(to me) one-third the sum of blue.
Tired of larger, more convincing elaboration, the dogs
light firecrackers beneath the breakfast table.

The father, stooping to retrieve his paintbrush, decides

today he gave blood for the wrong reasons,
today is a good day to retire.

—*for Brian Shapiro*

HIS BLOOD BE ON US

Let us pray for all
the items we should like to have.
Except for cleverness
it's all over. He just slipped and slipped with timidity
finer than strength. Like a brazen carbon
the intent is satiric but effective
in a dim room. I'm amused
you should feel, in the calm of the quiet of Sunday
a sense of something strange
hanging over you. The idea here
is glaring, given a fixed set
of circumstances and a certain individual end.
In the end it is a poor romancer
who cannot work out the result.

The sky is excellent. In a neighboring landscape
two young women in extravagant white finery
enter a once notorious dance hall.
Gratitude alone should compel us
for what now in the blue weather
shows signs of becoming settled.
He has come to us at last.

RATIONAL RATIONAL
God damn it, you've got to be kind. — Kurt Vonnegut

This war cannot be won.
The memory of the garden illusion caught me up
again in the turmoil, viewing my inner self
as an old person looking at distant scenery.
Add whenever the owner was asked to put on a demonstration.
When he gave the mule his first command.
Add the badly painted backdrop. Plus
my gaze to the left. It is not a good place to be,
to follow any verbal order you're given.
First you have to get my attention. Someone
somewhere is trying to get my attention.
The query came from somewhere inside me, quite gracefully.
Add tired. Tired, tired. Plus decide
what such-and-such really is. Add effective
tools in the war against so monstrous a wrong.
Add ideology superimposed on us during the course of our learning.
Add the maverick must be allowed to retreat
to his private domain and live in any manner
he finds rewarding. Add interminable
conversations with your cats. Plus
watching television all day long. Plus as long
as we don't interfere with the freedom
or well-being of any other person.
Plus easier enforcement will catch more criminals.
Plus the international politics of debt.
Add a lot of what I've been talking about
has to do with the other guy. Add more and more
companies are requiring pre-employment urine testing.
Not just bus drivers and firemen, add furniture salesmen.
Grocery store clerks. Add recipients of public housing,
university loans, or academic grants. Add veteran cops.
Add the daily
shaving of the head and body. Today verbal assurance
is acceptable, but what about tomorrow. Add tomorrow.

Add what extent do you feel it is justifiable
for someone else to control your personal behavior
if it contributes to the public benefit?
Add I have questions in one pocket and secrets in the other.
Add I've got nothing to hide.
To this delicious feeling of being alive add definition
of a police state, were it to quietly materialize around you.
Plus proportions of any serious effort to help those
with debilitating mental illnesses. Add children
who have no families, no food,
no education and no hope.
Plus interactive software.
Add we're a drag strip.
Remodeling experts.
Add redneck gangs with names like the Spookhunters.
Add panicky local authority.
Subtract modernism.
Add propaganda. Reasonable suspicion. Swift action.
If you are a person in authority,
you now don't have to confront the suspected wrongdoer;
you confront their possessions instead.
Add quick-witted reporters.
Add legislature. Boot camps.
To six-pack stucco tenements add weed-and-seed urban rescue.
Weary populations preoccupied with fantasies of becoming Byzantium.
Electrified teenagers of all classes.
Deceptive technology.
Add your personal limits.
Add our parents' permission.
The social burden of servicing the deficit.
Add comment.
I had a horrible nightmare
last night, far more intense than any dream I've had in years.
Add I was at a hotel. Add everything I owned was in the room.

Plus I'm naked.
This wonderful glow inside my being —
the expanse of green grass and the shimmering
leaves vibrating in the sunlight
making this a wonderful place
to sit and contemplate. Here is what happened.

—for Greg Purcell

pause

HIGH PARK

What is really happening in the brain is happening
                                in darkness.

It's theater time. My tinnitus is really out there
                                and there is no way of getting away from it.

After the letter reading was over, she asked me
                                if I would like to come out to the farm after work
                                on Friday, to stay the weekend.

Something was taking shape across the room. There was a sense
                                of gold somewhere in the red. The legs
                                of the red-painted kitchen table glowed,
                                and the room was alive with a soft light.

Twenty-four hours later I was talking again, sitting
                                on his brown leather couch, keeping silent
                                while he did things to his tape recorder
                                on the low table in front of me.

It's a sort of brother relationship — the brother neither of us had.

I didn't talk about my reason for being there. The flowers
                                were shimmering. The flowers on the curtain
                                were shimmering and we're holding hands
                                for the last time.

Walking up the street at midnight we approached a frail grandmother
                                who was pulling her grocery cart behind her,
                                talking on a cellular phone.

To be too thorough or specific about sensing possible let-downs
                                in a possible romance is to establish
                                a place for them in the subconscious mind.

We walked past a recommended Portuguese restaurant.
All attempts at smiling or sounding lighthearted
had been abandoned.

The continuation of the human species itself
obviously requires we get to work
very quickly.

The dimension behind the dizziness. Boy, I really felt that drink!
I may be sloppy, but let me explore the sexual. Wow.
I may be spacey in the head, but my body
knows where it's at.

It wasn't until I had reached the hotel, getting out of the cab
that I remembered the blue nightgown, and laughed.

The door opened and a mass of electrified silver hair poked itself
into my field of vision. Words carving through my mind
occasionally taking a wrong turn
through labyrinthine caverns.

I didn't even know I wanted cornbread with scallions until now.

Not to be too thorough or specific about sensing possible let-downs,
but you told me it would be a wonderful experience.

Her bluff is being called. The clouds are beginning to lift.
The sun is breaking through.

I sat on the couch for a long time, mentally replaying the conversation,
word by extraordinary word.

In the early evening, we gathered together for supper.

She didn't talk about my reason for being there. There used to be no limits
                    but now the State is with us continually.

He's a person, who, when he's attracted to someone,
                    intuitively senses what's lacking in
                    that person's emotional life. A compulsion
                    to become whatever they need most.

A few words are needed here regarding
                    the neurotransmitter serotonin. I don't excuse
                    the boredom. I want the boredom.

It wasn't very crowded, probably because of the rain,
                    but there were some patient, raincoated visitors
                    who were obviously used to this kind of weather.

It is in the head I am attentive.

I follow the unfolding of an inner experience
                    sculptured with moss-covered stone
                    and moving water. Subtle gradations of color in the pebbles.

Imagine a scientific expedition to a distant world. The continuation
                    of the human species itself
                    obviously requires we get to work.

Novel structures indicate novel processes.

The sight of the great seated Buddha on the path
                    above the garden pierces my heart.

So much for fame and sure method.
The meantime awaits without.
Possessions behind them, spirit before,
we are pleased to enter once more.
We Americans like big, but yours are quite different,
we assure you. These are wonderful too.
It is clear you caught the gesture of leaning against
the prominent, perfectly important.
I consider myself fortunate. There is room.
We will trust you in a country
that won't be named. It will be said I have tried
with inferior music. It will be said
I have tried without title and am unsure.

THIN RED LINE

After giving birth, she says, she dismissed the universe
                              and told it that it was
                              on its own.

Without my presence there will be no magic in your life.

Pretty intense, but okay.

Sometimes when you go through a miserable thing
                              you become allergic to everyone.

The nurturing mother reaches for her child's hand,
                              feeling with pleasure the texture of the skin
                              and the solid bones of the fingers.

She takes the grossest materials and blows them
                              into shimmering bubbles.

So we rejoice in the salvage. The afternoon and evening clouds
                              through the window at a specific moment.

As long as you stay off the piano keys.

And the I who thought I knew who I was woke up
                              tending the oyster bar.

He has no conscience because he has no need
                              of humility in his life. Somewhere, out there
                              in the shifting sands of Death Valley
                              is a nothing to repeat always —

Composed harmonies can be claustrophobic at first.
                              My recollection of the endless summer
                              is almost unbearable.

Tension between perception of reality and growing up
                              mesmerized me and my friends.

With the mirage of unattainable futures in the distance
                              it became urgent to wring as much
                              freedom from the night as possible.

Just a few minutes ago, I was looking out the living room window
                              and two dogs were playing
                              on the boulevard.

Actually I had a wonderful time. The only horse I bet on
                              was a winner despite narrow odds.

And it's just so fun to speculate, to play a role
                              in making a nature scene.

When the rival withdrew from the field
                              their faces showed confusion
                              or something like embarrassment.

Taking pleasure to strut around with a gun in your belt.

And it's just so fun to speculate —

In the kitchen, a soup was simmering on the stove.
                              On the tile counter were green lettuces and bright-
                              red tomatoes heaped into piles alongside loaves of bread.

I went through a few moments of seeing my worst faults.

Ceiling-high bookcases thrust into the room.

There was a central room, surrounded by a veranda
                              sloping downwards, outwards on all sides.

Of course it's not unthinkable that I've held several hands and waited
                         to cry and never cried but wanted to
                         but was filled with too much anxiety.

You're not obvious for saying it's dark and intolerable
                         outside. It's a soggy gray fucker

giving dignity and purpose to small rebellions —
                         the monotonous hot rod and beach
                         riots and motherly perspective.

It occurred to me that all I had to do was keep
my eyes open, focus on the body, the face
looking in. I learned not to
talk about that kind of thing, getting the idea I was different.
I'm reminded by your remark, smiling despite the effort
to seem sad. We could drift out into space so easily.
I'm saddened when any form of life is pushed out by people.
That's how I rehearse it, lying here.
Leaving for the party I giggled at my reflection in the mirror.
The proceedings took place in a large room with everyone sitting,
concentrating on what was being said about the value
of going through this horrible place. The money.
In the restaurant across the street
we sat and laughed out loud. Trying to remember
what it is to talk in the ordinary world.
Here for the departure.
Here for the accidental, the city-
to-city, trying to remember when
we lived here, the parties, the jargon,
the reassuring night. Reaching for facts,
something hard to pin down.
The money equally hard to pin down.
There was a reassuring night, like it was good to be home.
Learning not to talk about that kind of thing
we could drift out into space so easily.
Step down into the little room with its shelves and shelves
of everything. All children see the world this way
at a certain time. Last night was a beautiful gift.
My love, I just thought of something I might do.
When I returned from the porch
several others were seated at the table.
It was nearly dark and I'm still unsure of her
really being able to see me.
A monolithic identity. I was startled
by the server. Perceiving hostility

in faces looking at you — this is what you are seeing,
the people in the room, the laminated paper.
I couldn't let him go any further. Trying to remember
what it is to talk in the ordinary world.
He looked up at the big windows, then back at me.
I have a tendency to be sharp,
but you're the last person I want to hurt
in any way. Not that it's uninteresting, but I've never been
particularly satisfied with my dream life,
even when I'm flying.
I opened my eyes and blew air.
It occurred to me that all I had to do was keep
my eyes open, focus on the body.
There was a body to look at,
a face to look on, to focus on.
But floating upwards.

I love the smell of sauerkraut
in the morning. It smells like sauerkraut
in the morning.

RY COODER

Already he has recovered from what he has achieved.

He felt his first grade etchings neither identified
                  with the subject nor abandoned
                  eloquence. If not the whole of genius,
                  they at least appear to plunge forward.

Certain lovers suffer. There are always new phrases
                  popping up.

And the old people who already have stood an awful lot.

Purchasers may think with considerable enthusiasm, coolish in quality
                  so far from throwing overboard
                  standards must be allowed.

All of these latter will now be gratified.

Certain other lovers after that.

Circles being so closely allied, the cruder
                  the better. Consciousness is slight
                  anyway in public. To overload them
                  is not particularly necessary.

That I am myself a person. Looking at me, if posterity
                  were to peep with the naughty little
                  excessively insisted upon skill
                  of the present group.

There are times we don't care he is modified.

He is a hero.

Being somewhat furtive myself
                    I am quite willing to humor
                    the qualities of others.

Having reached a comparative period of calm
                    worthy of study. Only last night
                    by the time you reach the cab
                    stamped with a champagne hallmark.

CABBAGE ALLEY

What's so special
about the second line?

I've been
wondering how
things were going.

It seems as though
it will stand
forever and ever.

It was
a hard job,
but I've never
worked an easy one.

I thought you might
want to know.

I ask to see
this essence
in my surroundings,
enough to drop

my concerns about aging,
seeing clearly
that everyone
has as much
God as he
or she wishes.

Right now
the connection
escapes me.

Thank you
for these
materials.
Now I know
they are feelings.

The closeness and energy
among us
have grown
to powerful proportions.

The food is really good.

What had been my mountain
overlooking the
obvious reference.

I know
they are only feelings.

The extra
trick between the beats.

I am amazed
at how quickly
I can change
my feelings. Sometimes
I remember pleasant things
from childhood

which I had
completely forgotten.
Having a great time
with my guests.

With or without consent
it's going to proceed
in its own way.

Information comes
through the arms.

Our subconscious awareness
while doing the dishes,
turning out
the lights.

What can I say?

I'm growing kale
and tomato together
in the same
undersized pot
knowing they likely
won't become food.

When I take the time
to be still

and sick
of the world.

What are these
people cheering
for?

Becoming some
version of normal
through the confusion.

I miss
how the sunlight
filtered through
green leaves.

A beautiful poem
just fell over.

Hopefully the evening
won't.

It seems as though
it will stand
forever and ever.

We persuade
ourselves we're not
being confronted
by the removal
of a living
body of energy.

It was

motions and voice —

now we begin
to believe in it.

— for Jennifer Rupert and Chris Glomski

THE BEACH PATROL

There are precedents having to do
with matrimony, a cartilage spun
into cantilever with requisite handholding
and prayer. In view of the sunshine
imagined on your hair — the considered
steadiness of dreams
in the parking lot.
Real estate bows into
preventive wedding
coupled with — my fingers are blue and aching
and security is circling the obvious family.
I'm stuck near a river
I can feel the evidence of
but can't imagine. The bed degradation
is peculiar — self
(bio jammed with stuff to say)
realizing the unanswered
luck of Slavic innocence
between autumn and spring,
unaware of the boxed owl behind you.
I've never known you to pray this way,
exhausted and laudable, bristling by the sonar,
a satellite for the New World —
yellow in the vicinity of the trachea,
resonant hourglass and chronic twilight
alone with your governor device.

FLANGER

The processes of the artist are mysterious
                          and none can explain.

The longer you peer into the moonlit oceans
                          the more profound seem their depths.

There is something supreme too — terrifying,
                          dreamlike events.

Physicists consequently block the entrance.

His career on the whole was uneventful. (Smiling)
                          — who were his warm friends in a manner
                          of deep congratulation, perfectly innocent,
                          legitimate.

This is the real accusation against the times we live in.

But I prolong the lugubrious note unduly. There is no
                          rich person apparently. I'm sure proper
                          measurement was taken. One
                          remains on the telephone.

You are right with science in the theatrical world.

When I get to Europe I can attempt my theory,
                          cure my pains with an application of pure
                          color (or carroty rust.)

HARRY NILSSON

Now that I am a spaceman, nobody cares about me. — Harry Nilsson, "Spaceman"

The very next summer, on August 19th to be precise,
I went to the house of the young widow with two young children
who stood there holding their hearts in their hands.

There was a sign by the front door steps that said STARVE A RAT!
COVER YOUR GARBAGE!

It was ten years before I was married and I was working
twelve to fourteen hours a day, using Scott Turner's office to write
after getting off work at the bank.

When my uncle taught me how to sing, I understood
that was how he wanted me to be — masterful, confident, smiling,
sure.

And I shall wait in the rain and snow on the porch until you speak
and tell me to buy a trailer so we can go to Vegas
and be very happy.

Mickey Dolenz calls me the Harry ride.

Love is something you have to learn.

Get married at the Marriott
next to LAX. The priest beams down.

Beautiful Una, you were a virgin and I'd never had one.

I know you weren't crazy about the whole Randy Newman thing,
but it was better than the Smothers Brothers thing.

It occurred to me that if I thought only now, at this moment
in my life, of belonging to someone, it was because my hold
on life itself was endangered.

Mama Cass. Keith Moon. Historically doomed,
as you'd put it. But they were real people.

I'll never forget the shame I felt when she kissed our hands.
From that day onwards I've hated to see anyone
kissing someone's hands.

Never own a flat in London.

Note to self: Never trust a trusted friend with your money, but be someone
on whom nothing is wasted.

I drove a few miles in silence through the lunar valley,
mountains on both sides,
not yet desert but a coarse-grained prelude to it.

"Coconut". The comic "Coconut"— was in how many movies?
Fucking penance for *Popeye.*

Midnight Cowboy wasn't bad.

Fortune has a way of figuring you out.

It was the last night of our holiday and we stared
into an octagonal, palm-shaped pool glistening with black
rocks that slid and clicked — ah, ha! Turtles!

Love IS something you have to learn, like English.
English? No, Danish.

pause

THE DEAD C

The sea is violet, and it's an extraordinary thing to experience being helpless,
extraordinary to realize you have complete power over another person you can hurt,
thinking it's your turn to experience being helpless and it's the other who has to be aware of
the hidden, dark impulses, arrogance, added-up vulgarity,
and make a choice, whatever action or concern
she is busy with at the moment. We were due to perform — both of us —
to a roomful of people and I felt my face flushing. There was already a buzz.
She decided she wanted to be alone for a few minutes and went into the dining room
from where she could see the outside world in two directions:
through the big window to the mountain and through the sliding glass doors
to the patio and garden. God is everything that exists,
good and bad. There is this punk band I'd like to introduce you to. They're charming.
He'd grunt and say uh-huh like a delinquent kid, wobbling
at a point — some heavy-duty poltergeist — I mean, they must have thought
we were maniacs — this IS America — having to scream but with your mouth shut
and then it's your turn to experience being helpless.
After about fifteen minutes of handshaking and that smiling,
we were shown to another room and a small stage, the place where nothing makes sense
and yet everything makes sense, moving past this or that signature
without conscious thought — only the absence of a particular thing in the room
will make you notice — and the attention is to those parts of the room which involve
whatever action or concern one is busy with at the moment. In the penthouse
of the hotel, we were escorted into a room with large windows and a bar
where I was able to get a glass of water, and there we met
with the people who had come to manage us,
digressions right and left, and I must learn to keep my sense of humor.
I wanted to be alone for a few minutes, went into the dining room,
but still I could see the blur of his face in the shadows,
the shine of hair and beard, the observer keeping track.
You've just had your first glimpse of an aspect of my world I can't explain.
Of course, I thought all that male bonding was sexy. Full of fantasy
and an amusing fellow, cultured to the breaking point, and if it were not so mean
to keep pressing the point, last week when talking of the charming
and insufficiently appreciated earth and sky, I permitted myself to moralize
following a cooling bath of beer. The whole stage was covered in it

and we didn't know what to do when we started playing.
Those who knock most loudly at the door are least likely to be admitted —
and we didn't know what to do when we started playing.
Those who knock most loudly at the door are least likely to be admitted —
stealing his mother's jewelry, her clothes, her makeup, her scarves.
He knows we know, so we religiously close our lips. Slowly
the message is getting through though we don't have much to say.
There would be a stillness, a sense of time having stopped.
But at some point she's going to have to say, Okay, this is it;
I'm going, I wish you well, I'm sorry.
Eventually these words have to be said.
You're confusing the Hanging Gardens of Babel with the Tower of Babylon.
It's a common mistake, resolving to ignore the trunk of FUCK YOUS
and DON'T TAKE IT SO SERIOUSLY, ASSHOLES sitting at the bottom of your stomach,
acting as if only the present were real, and only tonight mattered —
then it occurred to me we might try a real challenge
if everyone can get onboard with the idea. In bed
after a couple of half-hearted attempts at lovemaking
we acknowledged it was a lost cause, curled up together
and went to sleep. Most of us who've managed to live
beyond twenty-five or thirty have got some cautionary voice that says *Hold it,*
Watch it. Is this person genuine; is he who he really seems to be?
I mean, like a physical blow to the body, it is actually painful.
And will you do me the kindness of warning me if you're going to do it
again, so I can leave the room?
Plus, I guess he liked her physically. I mean, they had the same kind of body structure.
It was pretty cut and dry. And cute. She was looking through a book of fairy stories
with illustrations by the great enchanter Arthur Rackham,
and everyone around her had been silent for a long time,
absorbed in their various interior worlds
when suddenly the room was jarred by a single, forceful note
struck on the piano. The color of music shuns representation.
People obliged to watch each step they take.
AND THIS IS AMERICA!
TELL US A STORY ABOUT LIFE IN THE ENCLAVES OF THE RICH!

REACH WITH YOUR HANDS INTO THE SKY!
Oh, we were a band of beauties.
She was also very pregnant, so we slept for a couple more hours
then dressed for the first obligation of our visit: meeting her family.
I wore a long, loose, white cotton dress with ruffles, comfortable
and relatively graceful glitter. The first lesson
was in the ways of greeting. Women are welcomed in the French manner
with a kiss on each cheek, kiss left then right; men
shake hands with men. The sentimental
will guarantee you a place in American heaven.

That it is amazing to realize
he is yet a celebrity. He says too
that certain Americans have failed
to appreciate him, that this is extraordinary.
One feels quite helpless to combat
so unreasonable a situation.
Arguing won't help. In fact
nothing can be done. Talking to them
won't help. Explaining
won't make them feel quite ashamed
for not really liking music.

THE SECOND HALF OF THE FLIGHT

Going on old gut instinct I said,
instead of pushing away your dead friends,
when you wake up try bringing them along
as allies during the day.
There was a smudge of blood on my collar, and I was staring at it
not really thinking anything at all when the roof fell in.
You don't often get to hear the actual words of an early childhood
programming. With new emotions creeping into your life
perhaps higher frequency is compensated
by reduced intensity. After the debacle
in San Fernando Valley, I told her she could do anything
she felt like — a simple gesture
to reassure the child inside. At the top of the hill
there was a crumbling cement overlook and the remnants
of a spiral staircase to an upper level
that no longer existed. The traveler can see
a legion of bulldozers developing
rapidly into the green — the millions
and millions of compounds that are known.
It is a project not a certainty. Christmas
in the hills, big smiles. The Russians recoil
from nothing, so I never try to urge an opinion.
Real caring, like love, cannot be forced,
and she should have sufficient insight of her own
to be aware of what her feelings toward me really are.
Trying to open my eyes
or lift a finger to deliver the most reassuring description.
Jesus Christ! There are foods
and metabolites, hormones, enzymes and minerals that in essence
define us. Like a mummy in an undiscovered tomb or a star
in some undescribed galaxy, they may be unknown to us,
but they might be present in a tea leaf, or a moss spore.
Not wanting to get in the way of the image, I speak quietly,
but at least now I can talk about it, looking at the way her body lay,
hands relaxed, fingers loosely curled at her sides.

I couldn't figure out how I got outside. The view
was lovely, surrounded by palm trees and flowering bushes
of many kinds, and it was the tropics, the real tropics,
again. I also teach hypnotherapy. I've written a book and I'm doing very,
very well. Would your dog fight a bear
for you? I'm thinking about this big zoom lens,
how I began exploring the world of administrative officialdom —
for ultimate, magical overlaps. The reward
for this caper will be in the stamps, not the science.
Bigger bridges. Better bones. The victim was Catholic.
A lot of intensity and passion and wonderful Latin phrases.
It's here that the two areas of my personal interest —
swamp collecting, GOD SAVING US — effectively overlap. A sherbert-cool breeze
coming through my open doors, to my immense relief.
I had been sweating in the earlier humid warmth, and now,
finally, I was feeling comfortable. Peace and quiet
for a while. He sat back in his seat, looking at me thoughtfully
during liftoff. That makes very much sense, as you say. It is true
I should not be afraid of them. Why should I fear dead friends
who love me?

— for John Beer

STARGAZING

Helicopters are the real trouble.
I dream of nothing but travelers who exit
trembling like me, not knowing
they've died. A reprisal,
I preoccupy the countryside. The real
occupants wear silver shovels
or anchors! The sky
is full of tinny stars and I love
two thirds of the world
I don't understand. My sweetheart
brings molecules and reads the sky out loud.
We should be satellites!
My nightmare about vacancy and life
should be more salient. The day grows
bluer, fetching a vision. November
brings excessive kinship, arriving
stiff-necked, wearing veils
cut from shopping bags. Staggering
as if a meteor collided, my mind
molders but still I witness my breaking
bones like terrible luggage
as the sky shudders,
turning into snow.

How do you recognize a lovely place?
The rotten anthropology of superheroes
hovers above the conference table, exhausted
on the idea of dazzling people. A plugged
organization of the moon like a turnpike
undecorated by barely legal children —
true stories end in the moody doctor city
but I always say the wrong thing. Away
from Las Vegas I spend too much time
at the whale facility. I'm bored with awakening
into historical X-rays
of the NO MOMENT. (What showmanship!)
Who does wear a cape underwater?
Now Egypt is miniaturized and it may never rain
again. Hurling bodies and collapsing lungs
used to be honestly scripted activities —
the stillness in the dream of important history.
From now on your stillness will be happening.
In the actual dream remember how the children
were modified, the sputtering, Russel Crotty language?
Friendly Calliope is no longer remedial
in the crisply American landscape. Even snowy
Vermont grows opaque, a diminished suggestion
in the desert mirror. I feel as if I'm speaking to a dear friend
but I'm saying the wrong things. *I don't like cockfights*
or *you'd rather be my daughter*, deeply, authentically
factualizing our especially Southern roots.

PENGUIN
Have you seen, have you seen magic shadows? — Fleetwood Mac, "Nightwatch"

My fugues have no apparent relation to past trauma of any kind.
When it came time to rehearse we decided to get glamorous.
We get all done-up for rehearsal. Gradually, imperceptibly, things begin
slipping back into their normal place. My body is slowly rotating
into its proper north-south orientation. My playing is flawless
as it turns out. The audience goes nuts
but what was it all about?
Had I longer to see the aspects and facets of the family,
which as we know are not always tickety-boo but I have drifted away
like a wide-winged bird over many things that are meaningless,
yet my mind is clicking away quite properly on other levels.
I was never in it for the money, but I see where it goes
without ever touching it.

It was like a honeymoon — nothing made sense, sounding utterly
convincing to my own ears — selfness in training, needing a month of good sleep.
When I woke I saw the sunlight streaming in across the ceiling and thought
oh boy, we were awful yesterday, the obvious response being
to phone the boss and tell him you're sick and go to bed until it's passed,
except Boss is in bed too.
Don't let the lack of his spirit blind your life.
You would expect me to tell you, wouldn't you, if our positions were reversed,
while I look for a suitable shirt, but you
don't have any more to accomplish, nothing at all.
Did you ever love me? Could I grit my teeth
and carry it all off without anyone being the wiser?

Any words that have concrete meanings are fine
and completely friendly. The whole history of the human race
is somewhat sad, wouldn't you say, if you look at it
in a certain way? But then, if you squint a bit differently
it isn't sad at all.

There were times we were all hurting really bad,
thinking the bed will win. Maybe it was the beginnings of trademark —
if we stayed telepathic we couldn't do that — surprise, surprise,
and that's how we decided to do the dance
and that's how The Dance came about.
There was a large, grassy clearing in the forest,
the trees around it thick and tall and there was sunlight
on the grass. We knew that people were worshipping
and the way they did it was to gather around a place like this
and allow themselves to become a part of it, greeting it
and letting it greet them feeding their bodies to their souls,
the pity of the tribe was how we imagined it,
seeing behind closed eyelids a lovely scene,
looking down from an open balcony into a central courtyard.
We were in a place that appeared to consist of baskets of flowers.

I could see only the top of his brown hair and his moving hands.
There's a lot of color. It's more noticeable than usual — I mean
there are little prisms, rainbows everywhere
but whether it was guitar or piano I couldn't tell you — this is
pre-Lindsey. The back room was vicious, everyone on a different drug.
If you turned your back you'd better keep on walking.
We did this every night, playing country rock at the height of glitter,
mixed-bag material. We needed theoretical problems!
My back to him, I said, "You mean us poor, sad little cast-offs,
wouldn't it be nice if we could cheer each other up
so our miser wouldn't cast a pall
on the happiness of the Prince and Princess?"
Only I'm foreshadowing with picky surfaces.
The morals are contemporary — argument
of sounds, accomodation, implosion, but still
the ineffable grace of seeming perishable —
the ordinariness of making love and hearing music.

I'm okay by myself, believe me.
It's a thought that gives rise to immense self-compassion. Okay,
I'll deal with this.
I kind of went on the skids.
It was just the four of us finally starting to crank it out, faster
and faster, until it was too fast.
Then one day, it was a Friday, always payday and I was in the bedroom
beginning to sort out what I thought of as my shitpile,
a collection of such things as dresses, belts, stockings, photographs,
and old magazines all waiting to be put where they belong.

HOME WITH LIGHT AND NEUTRAL BLOSSOMS

Between fitting home with light and neutral blossoms
while prairie continues uncollected,
how do you recognize a lovely place?
In some intervals green is less obtuse,
can't wait to embrace some sparrow
part of the season. Nor pretending
with dated foregrounds, recollection
as it seems to witness in gradual glitter
as it seems to recollect, can barely wait
to incorporate. Of the few hovering people
who belay the world with argument,
who, legitimizing flora, pretend a fashion
gradually. And gladly seeking to describe
of all the people and methods of green
to the shape of your embrace
all light is mechanical, another interval
gladly seeking to describe a method.

IF HE WAS FROM VENUS, WOULD HE FEED US WITH A SPOON?
— The Replacements, "Alex Chilton"

The chords are such colors as pleased the artist,
and that is the reason, I think, they now please others.
The more I think about it, the more miffed I am
that I wasn't asked to that party. Good grief,
why am I being treated like a baby? A lot of work
gets done here, and a lot of magic has happened
in this place over the years. He loves it;
he really loves this room and what he's done in it.
When it came, the sound from his throat was strangled
as if he had come to the end of some strange, exhausting battle.
The most sacred things carry us beyond words.
The story of a major alteration of consciousness that occurred because,
apparently, it was time for it to happen.
I had the impression that some corner of his soul
was still attached to wherever he'd been,
but the ties were weakening. We clustered around him
in chairs and on the floor. He'd launch into us
about our appearances. Everything you do,
it seems like you strive for anonymity.
Thank you, I said, reaching up and stroking the side of his cheek.
I feel horrible for all of his women. There were no other girls
to hang out with, believe me, it was mostly guys
and the few women that were there
didn't really know they were women.
It's hard to believe I've finally met somebody who's trying
all of these things, exploring the universe, and isn't afraid
of discovery, when most people want just to make enough money
to support families and house payments, and buy the usual nice things.
For years and years I've been fascinated by this whole idea
of experience, of exploration, and I've read Huxley and Michaux
and anybody else I could find who seemed to know anything about it.
I kept gazing at him, trying not to let my happiness show.
It was a rare thing for me to be feeling so happy.
I had long ago figured out the conflicts involved in trying

to clear up any accumulation of objects that represented
some part of myself, especially an unwanted part.
But that wore off pretty quickly. There are coordination problems
with the fingers, a few little odd neurological signs that bear watching.
What am I doing to my body? When I first started performing
I got a kind of thrill out of it. I had exactly what I wanted.
There were mornings when I felt like the king
of the world. I'd imagined myself
into my life. Everything you do — it seems like you strive
for anonymity. I like to think, because of my unlimited talent
I would've risen back to the top and been recognized
sooner or later anyway, but that's not necessarily true.
Basically, I have one feeling — the desire
to get out of here. Do you want me to quit, or do you want
rock and roll? One of the problems in talking
about this kind of exploration is vocabulary.
There simply aren't the right words available, words
everyone can agree on to do a good job of defining
this territory. We got chased all the same. These fucking rednecks
just came out of a truck and started shooting at us. There was this law
in Memphis, where if your hair touched the top of your ears
you could be arrested for being a homosexual. I remember
not having any sort of feeling of anything but verbal aggression.
I had no feeling of physical aggression. Do you want rock and roll,
or do you want me to quit? We clustered
around him, in chairs and on the floor. He'd launch into us
about our appearances. Decorate the tree, kids!
I have come to appreciate, at a very deep level,
the possibility that this state (blessedly transient),
might be the day-to-day reality of some guy out there
on the street. The house is dominated by its three-storey
living room and impressive fireplace, built out of impressive dark stone
and volcanic rock. From the outside,
this was an impressive-looking A-frame house.

The windows were immense, allowing a view of trees
and the Mississippi which flowed past us.
There was no insulation anywhere. We were cold
all the time.

pause

THE GREEN LANTERN PRESS

Founded in 2005, The Green Lantern Press is an artist-run, non-profit press focused on emerging or forgotten texts in order to bridge contemporary experience with historical form. We celebrate the integration of artistic mediums. We celebrate the amateur, the idealist and those who recognize the importance of small independent practice. In a cultural climate where the humanities must often defend themselves, we provide intimate examples of creative thought.

Dedicated to the "slow media" approach, The Green Lantern Press conceives each book as a curatorial site; small editions are printed with artist plates, ephemeral inserts and silk screen covers. We are efficient about the material we use, economic about our proportion and intent on local production.

To step beyond the bounds of a single book, the press is partnered with The Paper Cave—a for-profit bookstore—and The New Corpse—a salon-style performance space—in order to support artists, writers, discourse and community. These relationships form alternative and sustainable models for the presentation and distribution of contemporary art.

HIP HOP APSARA by Anne Elizabeth Moore w/ color plates supplied by author and silkscreen covers by Angee Lennard. Printed in an edition of 500, 2012. $20

KORDIAN by Juliusz Słowacki, translated from Polish for the first time by Gerry Kapolka, w/ silkscreen covers by Aay Preston-Myint. Printed in edition of 500, 2011. $20

LOVE IS A CERTAIN FLOWER by Stephanie Brooks, w/ color plates supplied by author. Printed in edition of 250, 2009. $10

LUST & CASHMERE by A.E. Simns, w/ library card inserts by author, miniature hand-knit sweaters by Kellie Porter, and silkscreen covers by Alana Bailey. Winner of 2008 IPPY Independent Voice Award. Printed in edition of 500, 2007. $20

THE MUTATION OF FORTUNE by Erica Adams, w/ color plates supplied by author and silkscreen covers by Aay Preston-Myint. Printed in edition of 500, 2011. $20

THE NORTH GEORGIA GAZETTE reprint of original 1821 newspaper w/ excerpts from Captain Parry's log, and supplementary contemporary texts by John Huston and Lily Robert-Foley. Color plates by Daniel Anhorn, Deb Sokolow, Rebecca Mir and Jason Dunda, w/ silkscreen covers and limited edition 7" record provided by Nick Butcher. Printed in edition of 250, 2009. $30

ON MARVELLOUS THINGS HEARD by Gretchen E. Henderson, introduction by G.C. Waldrep, w/ color plates supplied by Carrie Gundersdorf. Printed in edition of 500, 2011. $12

PALM TREES by Nick Twemlow, introduction by Robert Fernandez, w/ 125 limited edition dust jackets silkscreened by Sonnenzimmer. Printed in an edition of 500, 2012. $15

A SEASON IN HELL by Arthur Rimbaud, translated by Nick Sarno, w/ color plates by Gerry Bacasa and cardstock silkscreen covers by Sonnenzimmer. Printed in edition of 500, 2009. $20

SERVICE MEDIA: IS IT "PUBLIC ART" OR IS IT ART IN PUBLIC SPACE? edited by Stuart Keeler, introduction by Carol Becker and silkscreen covers by Angee Leenard. Printed in and edition of 500, 2012. $20

SO MUCH BETTER by Terri Griffith, w/ color plate by Zoe Crosher and silkscreen covers by Nick Butcher of Sonnenzimmer. Nominated for 2009 Lambda Literary Prize. Printed in edition of 500, 2009. $20

TALKING WITH YOUR MOUTH FULL ESSAYS by Lori Waxman, Claire Pentecost & Carrie Lambert-Beattie, edited by Elizabeth Chodos. Printed in edition of 250, 2008 $10

URBESQUE A COLLECTION OF SHORT STORIES by Moshe Zvi Marvit, printed in edition of 500, w/ silkscreen covers by Mat Daly, 2006. $20

THE WHITE HOUSE by Joel Craig, introduction by John Beer, w/ 125 limited edition dust jackets silkscreened by Sonnenzimmer. Printed in an edition of 500, 2012. $15

WRITING ART CINEMA 1988–2010 by Stephen Lapthisophon, introduction by Devin King. Printed in an edition of 250, 2011. $10

BOOKS PUBLISHED W/ THREEWALLS

ARTISTS RUN CHICAGO multiple contributors including Bad at Sports, Britton Bertran, Dan Gunn, Mary Jane Jacob, Allison Peters-Quinn, Temporary Services and Lori Waxman. Printed in edition of 500, 2009. $20

PAPER & CARRIAGE VOLS. 1, 2 & 3, multiple contributors including Brooke Anderson, Dan Beachy-Quick, Jesse Ball, Elisa Bogos, Lilli Carré, Henry Darger, Daniel Johnston, Peter Orner, Mattathias Schwartz, and Kate Zambreno, w/ silkscreen covers by Dan MacAdam of Crosshair, Sean Stuckey and Dan Wang. Vol 1 nominated for Utne Reader Award, Best New Publication. Printed in limited editions of 250, 2008. $18/ea.

THE PHONEBOOK VOL. 01 & 02, GUIDEBOOK edited by Caroline Picard, Nick Sarno and Shannon Stratton. Printed in an edition of 500, 2006-2008. $10

JOEL CRAIG lives and works in Chicago, Illinois. He co-founded and curates the Danny's Reading Series, and is the poetry editor for *MAKE: A Literary Magazine*.

JOHN BEER is the author of the poetry collection *The Waste Land and Other Poems* (Canarium, 2010).